ARCHITECTURE & DESIGN LIBRARY

RETRO MODERN

• ARCHITECTURE & DESIGN LIBRARY •

RETRO MODERN

Lisa Skolnik

A FRIEDMAN/FAIRFAX BOOK

Friedman/Fairfax Publishers

15 West 26th Street

New York, NY 10010

Telephone (212) 685-6610

Fax (212) 685-1307

Please visit our website: www.metrobooks.com

Library of Congress Cataloging-in-Publication Data

Skolnik, Lisa.
    Retro modern / Lisa Skolnik.
        p. cm. -- (Architecture and design library)
    Includes bibliographical references and index.
    ISBN 1-56799-917-4
    1. Modernism (Art)--United States. 2. Architecture, Modern--20th century--United States. 3. Furniture--United States--History--20th century. I. Title. II. Series.

N6512.5.M63 S56 2000
724'.6--dc21

                                                                99-053877

Editor: Hallie Einhorn
Art Director: Jeff Batzli
Designer: Jennifer O'Connor
Photography Editor: Valerie E. Kennedy
Production Manager: Camille Lee

Color separations by Colourscan Overseas Pte. Ltd.
Printed in Hong Kong by Midas Printing Limited

1 3 5 7 9 10 8 6 4 2

Distributed by Sterling Publishing Co., Inc.
387 Park Avenue South
New York, NY 10016-8810
Orders and customer service: (800) 367-9692
Fax: (800) 542-7567
E-mail: custservice@sterlingpub.com
Website: www.sterlingpublishing.com

To Howard, who first opened my eyes to an entirely new aesthetic twenty years ago
and still does so to this day.

Thank you to the talented and diligent staff at Michael Friedman Publishing Group, particularly
my editor, Hallie Einhorn. I am grateful for both her persistence in obtaining exceptional pictures
and her circumspect editing, which made the text as flawless as possible.

Contents

INTRODUCTION

Living was simpler in the 1950s, when the typical family had one television, one telephone, one record player, one bathroom, and one wage earner. There were no entertainment centers loaded with audiovisual equipment, no microwaves, no luxurious master baths, and no personal computers. But many of these modest, unassuming homes were filled with the furnishings of the period. Approximately half a century later, those pieces, and the homes they graced, became icons of twentieth-century design.

Today, midcentury modern architecture and furnishings evoke potent nostalgia in many and inspire intense passion in some who weren't even alive at the time. Many people prefer this style to the designs prevalent today and collect originals with which to furnish their homes, while others scoop up the often pricey reproductions, satisfied just to achieve the right look. And many architects and designers still take their cues from the aesthetic of the era, offering up works that pay homage to the period but have a decidedly contemporary twist.

At the time they were first made, these furnishings and the homes in which they took up residence merely represented the trends of the day. Open-plan ranches, split-level houses, and boxy apartment buildings were punctuated with lots of windows but were devoid of almost all ornamentation on the inside. This type of setting was the perfect stage for showcasing the bold but spare furnishings of the time. Hallmarks include such pieces as low-slung sofas covered in nubby fabrics, sculptural coffee tables, curvy chairs, and lanky tables in organic shapes. Also popular were whole walls of utilitarian but attractive shelving made of metal, plastic, glass, and wood—materials that sometimes appeared alone, but more often than not turned up in inventive combinations.

Breaking with tradition, these stylish furnishings were streamlined, lightweight, and often economical. Some pieces were created by top architects and designers, while others were the generic products of manufacturers. But almost all of the offerings were sparely elegant and sophisticated. And no matter how high or low or avant-garde

OPPOSITE: *The great thing about modernist pieces is that they often work well together, regardless of pedigree. In this inviting living room, such sterling pieces as Alvar Aalto's 1932 Paimio chair (foreground) and a 1946 Eames molded plywood chair (back, left) mingle with generic pieces of the period to stunning effect.*

these pieces looked, they all reflected modernism—the groundbreaking style that forever changed our conceptions of furniture design and architecture.

The basic philosophy of modernism was to blend functionalism and frugality. The style has its roots in events that occurred, and concepts that developed, around the dawn of the twentieth century. Many of its influences came from Europe. One such forerunner was the Vienna Secession, a movement that emanated from the desire of architects and designers to move beyond the design constraints of the past. Out of this group came architect Josef Hoffmann, who, in 1903, founded the Wiener Werkstätte (Vienna Workshops), the original goal of which was to promote utility and simplicity in furniture design. At about the same time, the Arts and Crafts Movement, which held that good design should be simple, well crafted, and available to all, was flourishing in England, the United States, and Germany. In Germany, where the style was called the Werkbund, emphasis was placed on the use of machines, and the primary goal was to create a new and much higher standard for industrial design. Architects and designers staged impressive exhibitions in Cologne in 1914 and Stuttgart in 1927 that had tremendous impact on the development of modernism.

The first few decades of the twentieth century also brought immense social, economic, and political changes, culminating in World War I and the Great Depression. In many parts of Europe, including Italy, Germany, Austria, Russia, and the Scandinavian countries, people began to question traditional norms and embrace utopian ideas. Movements that started in these countries attempted to put the dreams of the age into concrete form through the designs of buildings and furniture. The Dutch De Stijl, Russian Constructivism, German Bauhaus, and Italian Rationalism and Futurism movements attempted to integrate all the visual arts into architecture and design. Affordable furniture and functional housing for broad sectors of the population became an important concern, and designers rose to the task. Buildings were designed with clean lines and simple interiors. Despite initial goals, though, these structures weren't always inexpensive, and neither were the furnishings. Many architects and designers employed spare yet luxurious materials to fabricate their creations.

By 1930, what was then called modern architecture was popular in Europe and known in the United States. And in 1932, it took on a new name, International Style, which stemmed from an exhibition mounted at the Museum of Modern Art (MOMA) in New York City by Philip Johnson and Henry-Russell Hitchcock. The show was called "Modern Architecture: International Exhibition," and the accompanying book was entitled *International Style: Architecture since 1922*.

For the most part, the United States only watched while modern architecture swept across Europe. In American cities, skyscrapers were still erected with Gothic or Renaissance ornamentation, and most furniture was made in traditional styles or imported from Europe. But there was one notable designer in the United States who helped to push modernism forward during these early years. Russel Wright created the innovative, though boxy, Modern Living line for the Conant Ball Company in 1935. The pieces were made of solid maple, moderately priced, and sold individually instead of in complete suites, giving buyers the flexibility to arrange their own groupings. The line also featured the first mass-produced sectional sofa.

Although the International Style had spread quickly in Europe, there were factors working against it. Conservative forces were regrouping and acquiring political power. In Germany, Hitler perceived modernism as subversive and closed the Bauhaus School, leaving the neoclassicism of Albert Speer to spawn grandiose monumental buildings. Ludwig Mies van der Rohe, Walter Gropius, Marcel Breuer, and other noted German architects and designers fled the Nazi regime to teach at universities in the United States. Only in Italy did the powers in control allow designers to pursue their modernist ideals and continue their work.

Because of the political climate in most of Europe, there was a demise in modern architecture and furniture design in the 1930s, and the movement was totally interrupted there by World War II. However, around this time the International Style began to blossom in the United States, despite such hardships and obstacles as material shortages and manufacturing restrictions.

Architects and designers in the United States started to create streamlined houses and furnishings. They got some help from the most powerful quarters of the art community, including the Museum of Modern Art in New York. Founded in the early 1930s, this institution proved to be a pivotal influence in the development of design by sponsoring competitions and shows for innovative furnishings. These exhibitions stimulated the talented architects and designers of the era, and attracted worldwide attention.

One such MOMA show, a 1940 contest and subsequent exhibition entitled "Organic Design in Home Furnishings," was cosponsored by Bloomingdale's department store and is credited with changing the very face and nature of the U.S. furniture industry. The contest was intended to discover new talent and nurture seminal design, and it succeeded. Charles Eames and Eero Saarinen, two relatively unknown young architects associated with the Cranbrook Academy outside Detroit, took top honors in both categories—storage and seating—and brought about revolutionary changes in furniture design.

The chairs the duo created were sinuous and sculptural with fluid, three-dimensional shapes that rejected the right angle. They were also technologically innovative, using plywood in a completely new way. Layers were pressed into curves that hugged the body while supporting the spine, and these shapes set the stage for what was to come in the postwar period. The storage units were equally innovative, with mix-and-match groupings that had interchangeable drawers and doors. Both of these architects went on to ally themselves with furniture manufacturers and became leaders in the modern design movement.

Eames signed on with Herman Miller, while Saarinen's designs were produced by Knoll. Although neither company was well known at the time, both went on to become prominent manufacturers.

With the end of World War II, a demand for consumer goods was unleashed—and the U.S. furniture industry was ready. The period from 1945 to the late 1950s was a heyday for modern architects, furniture designers, and manufacturers alike. The building and furniture industries prospered because there was a need for new housing, as well as furniture to go with it, to accommodate all the couples who were marrying and starting families. And these industries had everything going for them—top designers to create new product; new technologies to make it

ABOVE: *Le Petit Confort was designed by Le Corbusier, Charlotte Perriand, and Pierre Jeanneret. The chair presented a radical change in that it turned the support system inside out, with the tubular metal forming a cage for the stuffed cushions. Having debuted in 1928, this classic design is still in production today.*

easier to build homes or fabricate pieces; a growing magazine industry to promote them; and an affluent public eager to buy.

Competition soon drove prices down, and homes and diverse lines of modern furnishings became available for every budget. Those who could afford to do so had architect-designed homes filled with the best name pieces of the era, while those who couldn't were able to buy knockoffs. Of course, taste was also a factor, and there were plenty of derivative designs that pandered to those who preferred busier pieces. Many manufacturers produced kitschy lines that employed some of the basics of modern design, but bore inappropriate ornamentation. Eventually, all the cheap and adulterated copies distilled the significance of the modern movement and helped lead to its decline.

As the 1950s drew to a close, the pendulum of American styles swung back to more mainstream designs, and Knoll and Herman Miller turned to producing contract pieces. But modernism did not die with the end of the 1950s, thanks to the Europeans, who took the underlying principles in new directions.

In Northern Europe, Scandinavian firms won acclaim for designs that adapted and softened the International Style with traditional Scandinavian values. Pieces in this vein continued to be produced throughout the 1960s. Teak Style wood furniture was also developed and coveted in Denmark and Finland because, after the suffering and deprivation brought on by the war, people longed for the warmth and security of these strong, blocky pieces with their textural upholstery. In Sweden, after World War II, the government began an educational campaign to spread the principles of modern living throughout the country and opened its own furniture-making shops. A number of successful nonprofits were also established to manufacture and distribute inexpensive furnishings, completely skipping over retailers.

It was Italy, though, that took the lead in furniture innovations as the International Style started to ebb. The designs embodied a new aesthetic approach, embracing sculptural solutions and countering the rigorous functionalism of the International Style, while taking the needs of broad sections of the population into consideration. Plus, designers in Italy were beginning to experiment with plastics.

Ultimately, the late 1960s, 1970s, and 1980s brought a new perspective to architecture and furniture design in both the United States and Europe. This style became known as postmodernism. It was a reaction to the functionalism and austerity of the preceding decades, and it employed new and experimental uses of colors, materials, and design. Since this period was a time of great prosperity, many architects and designers chose to create highly individualistic and extravagantly imaginative homes and furnishings. Others simply embraced all that was opulent and exorbitantly expensive.

Eventually, the excesses of the 1980s brought styles back toward modernism, or at least a sleeker and more minimal approach to home design. A growing desire to pare down possessions and simplify lives began to manifest itself.

In recent years, the trend has been to create more nurturing and tranquil environments—places in which to escape the high-tech tools that have overrun our homes and the heavy workloads that have encroached on our time. Modernism is seen as a style that can be applied or redefined to meet these needs. And correctly so, as the pictures on the following pages show. For, in actuality, the style that we know as modernism is so elementary and uncomplicated, but at the same time so eloquent and sophisticated, that it is the perfect vehicle for bringing balance to our fast-paced lives.

ABOVE: *These two icons of midcentury design, the Shell rocker and the Butterfly chair, are both graceful and powerful in their simplicity. The Butterfly chair was designed in 1938 by three Argentinean architects— Jorge Hardoy, Antonio Bonet, and Juan Kurchan—who had been inspired by a nineteenth-century British officer's folding chair. The Shell chair, designed by Charles Eames in the early 1950s, was available with different bases.*

ABOVE: *Architect Richard Neutra helped introduce modernism and the International Style to California. In such a balmy climate, a glass house that opened to the world outside made sense. Although this Los Angeles–area hillside home was designed by Neutra in the 1960s, its clean lines, open expanses, and celebration of nature make it equally enticing today.*

A B O V E : *Inside this same house, the hearth appears to be floating above the ground, in keeping with the home's airy quality. The wooden pillar to the left is actually built-in cabinetry, its flush doors inconspicuously keeping all sorts of clutter at bay. The living room is fittingly decorated with modern furnishings, including a George Nelson Coconut chair (1956), an Eames coffee table (1946), and an Eero Saarinen pedestal table (1956).*

CHAPTER ONE

THE LEANER HOME

Nestled among the colonials, Victorians, and Cape Cods that populate North American neighborhoods are numerous ranch houses and split-levels—the sorts of homes that have a plain facade, plenty of rectangular windows, a basement rec room, and an attached garage. In fact, some neighborhoods are composed entirely of these structures. These are the homes spawned in the post–World War II period by modernism, and hard as it is to fathom, they are nearly eligible for listing on the National Register of Historic Places.

Prior to World War II, modernism had gained acceptance in Europe, but only when Austrian architects Rudolph Schindler and Richard Neutra moved to the United States in the 1920s did modernism start to gain momentum west of the Atlantic. Schindler even worked briefly for Frank Lloyd Wright, who was advocating doorless, free-flowing interiors during the first decade of the century. Schindler and Neutra became partners in 1926 and opened their own firm in California, an area that proved to be especially receptive to modernism. They were followed in the 1930s by German architects Walter Gropius, Ludwig Mies van der Rohe, and Marcel Breuer.

These talented professionals designed groundbreaking homes that sported what would become the hallmarks of modernism: open-plan layouts, flat roofs, clerestory windows, cantilevered rooms, sliding glass doors, wraparound corner windows, interiors devoid of moldings and trim, and low-slung attached garages. These homes were cunningly situated on spacious, beautifully landscaped lots in ways that emphasized the views and took advantage of the light. Not surprisingly, these structures were first introduced and named in California, where architects were inspired by both modernism and the one-story Spanish ranchos of the American Southwest.

But many modern homes that had, and continue to have, a real impact on how we live were not designed by leading architects.

OPPOSITE: *Many modernist architects sought to blur the distinction between a home's interior and the surrounding land. With its sliding glass doors and floor-to-ceiling windows, this house, designed by Richard Neutra in 1956, makes the most of the tranquil setting and offers an unobstructed view.*

Instead, they emanated from developers who bought up vast amounts of farmland and built whole towns of identical houses, using prefabricated components and assembly-line methods. For instance, between 1947 and 1952, Levitt and Sons, an infamous developer of the period, constructed 17,000 such houses in a Long Island potato field that came to be known as Levittown. These were one-story ranch houses and hybrid split-levels, the latter having a second level on a portion of the house.

The new horizontal structures placed emphasis on efficiency and function, as well as informality and comfort. With open plans that merged kitchens and living or dining rooms, these homes promoted a more casual lifestyle. They had lots of large, horizontal picture windows, sliding glass doors, and patios secluded in the backyard, all of which were geared toward the notion that life should be lived both inside and outside the home. Houses were designed to eke out the maximum living space from the least amount of square footage. Highly practical and cost-effective, these homes also permitted shorter plumbing lines and heating ducts, eliminated or minimized stairs and the dead space created by landings and halls, and allowed easy access to the outdoors.

OPPOSITE: *Modernist architects often employed concrete in the homes they created. In this San Francisco house by Richard Neutra, the concrete is joined by rectangular picture windows, also characteristic of the style. The home is poised to take advantage of the waterfront view.*

ABOVE: *Walter Gropius's own home, built in the late 1930s, epitomizes the International Style, which rejected historical influences in favor of simple, geometric forms devoid of superfluous embellishments. It has all the benchmarks of modernism, including a flat roof, bands of horizontal windows, and an undecorated facade. The projecting mesh porch emphasizes the desire to incorporate nature into everyday living.*

OPPOSITE: *With concrete planes projecting at right angles over each other above a waterfall, Fallingwater, the Pennsylvania home designed by Frank Lloyd Wright in 1935, displays a powerful integration of landscape and structure. Ironically, Wright would not endorse the International Style, but his earlier open-plan designs inspired many architects who did.*

ABOVE: *The use of steel and concrete as structural elements made load-bearing walls unnecessary and facilitated the use of large expanses of glass. Ludwig Mies van der Rohe was a pioneer of this development, and his Farnsworth House was completed in 1951. Many years later, the interior was appropriately outfitted in spare pieces that Mies designed.*

ABOVE: *Although Mies van der Rohe's Farnsworth House was already under way at the time, architect Philip Johnson, who worked for Mies, built the first completed steel and glass house in 1949. Appropriately named the Glass House, the boxlike structure clearly emulates Miesian design.*

OPPOSITE: *The ideal midcentury ranch home set up the outdoors as an architectural detail in its own right. In this elegant version of the style, cedar planks have been used to articulate the roofline and to form a deck, bringing the outside into the actual footprint of the home.*

OPPOSITE: *Not every ranch house clings strictly to the tenets of modernism. Even though the style calls for a flat roof, a pitched version that allows rain to run off is much more practical.*

RIGHT: *Modernism was so universally accepted by the 1960s that it became mainstream. Ultimately, it provoked a reactionary style: postmodernism. This house blends a bit of both. Its horizontal lines and large picture windows overlooking the yard are pure modernism, while the detailing, construction materials, and bold colors are postmodern.*

ABOVE: *With its low-slung, flat base and horizontally oriented windows, this house, which architect Robert Venturi designed for his mother in the early 1960s, is not inconsistent with modernism. However, Venturi distorted the scale of the place by adding such exterior details as moldings, an oversize, avant-garde doorway, and a pitched roof. The structure proved that the principles of modernism could be taken in new directions.*

ABOVE: *Technological advances that permitted experimentation with shapes, scale, and multiple levels played a large part in the reinvention of modernism. In this 1960s beach house, cubic, sculptural forms are piled on top of one another in a balanced manner.*

LEFT: *Windows that wrap around corners are one of the most dramatic innovations employed in midcentury modern homes. Here, the device is taken a few steps further: these "windows" are actually sliding glass doors that open onto a peaceful patio. The second story is clad in translucent glass panels that enable the interior to garner as much natural light as possible.*

RIGHT: *Abstract and cubic designs that build upon the basics of modernism continue to be constructed today. While this contemporary home employs an abundance of glass and blends harmoniously with the landscape, its various levels and angled balconies demonstrate an evolution in architectural design.*

CHAPTER TWO

ROOM DESIGN

The midcentury modern room was essentially democratic; whether situated in an apartment or a house, it was unpretentious and free of the purely decorative architectural detailing that gives other styles their identities. The singular architect-designed homes of the day incorporated striking, but hardly lavish, materials, such as burnished wood for wall panels, rugged stone for hearths, and lustrous terrazzo. Such houses also made greater use of the period's characteristic architectural features, such as clerestory windows, vast picture windows, sliding glass doors, and sophisticated hearths. But overall, the typical midcentury room usually let the building materials, the furnishings, and the natural world outside its windows take center stage rather than showcasing intricate architectural features.

Midcentury modern rooms were not necessarily confined to the conventional geometric layouts that were the norm in prior generations of homes. The contained foyer was a thing of the past; instead, most of the main living areas were visible from the front door. Kitchens ambled around corners and assimilated breakfast nooks; living rooms flowed into dining areas and seemed to have interminable proportions thanks to floor-to-ceiling windows; and rec rooms or dens, with their meandering footprints, defined areas for different activities, from sewing to playing Ping-Pong to watching television. Only bedrooms and bathrooms remained relatively the same—smallish and straightforward, relegated to the back of the house or to the level above the rec room.

OPPOSITE: *Built-in furniture was often employed in the midcentury room, since it provided a way to keep the space open and free of clutter. Both shelving and seating lent themselves easily to this device, as demonstrated in the living area pictured here. Le Corbusier furnishings complete the period look of the space, which still has a lot to offer in contemporary times. Thanks to its classic, pared-down lines, the room provides a refreshing break from the sensory overload of today's busy world.*

The main living areas of the home saw the most change. Gone were the picture windows facing the street, the layers of molding rimming the walls, the fireplaces accentuated by stately mantels, and the tall, dignified doorways. Instead, living rooms and dining rooms typically flowed into one another without any walls to define their boundaries. Plus, these areas were often oriented toward the backyard to provide a better view. These gathering places were also outfitted in an array of natural-looking materials. For instance, it was commonplace to have whole walls clad in brick or stone.

Kitchens were also reinvented, mutating from clunky workhorses into sleek environments where efficiency and style coalesced. Some were self-contained but harbored the ubiquitous breakfast nook of the time, while others opened onto family rooms or even semiformal dining areas. Both situations often included "floating panels," which were basically abbreviated screens that delineated the different areas. Cabinets and appliances took on a more streamlined demeanor, and storage became more specialized. Individual cabinets were often adapted to accommodate specific items, such as pots and pans, dishes, or foodstuffs. Some kitchens were also outfitted with concealed counters that swung open or folded out for additional working or eating space.

But it was possible to achieve a midcentury look in more traditional homes with the right stuff. A stone hearth or a flagstone floor added plenty of modern panache to a space, as did the other popular materials of the day, such as colored or patterned linoleum and Formica, frosted glass, sleek wood or fiberglass panels, and textured, fibrous wall coverings. Whole banks of storage with a built-in appearance could be added to a room, thanks to a plethora of systems developed at the time. Ultimately, rooms were treated much like blank slates, which could be altered at will to fulfill changing needs.

ABOVE: *Space-efficient built-in shelves and a modernist hearth sans mantel provide a subdued backdrop in this living room. The chaise longue was designed in 1928 by Le Corbusier, Charlotte Perriand, and Pierre Jeanneret.*

ABOVE: *Postmodern spaces often take their cues from modernism, and this playful living room is a perfect example. While it has the floor-to-ceiling windows and low-slung hearth of a ranch house, the main support wall curves subtly and sports a bold shade of blue. Midcentury classics, such as Marcel Breuer's Isokon lounge chair (1935), a Mies van der Rohe couch (1930), and Le Corbusier's Le Petit Confort (1928), mingle with an angled postmodern cabinet attached to the wall.*

ABOVE: *Frank Lloyd Wright's Fallingwater has much in common with the precepts of the International Style. While the exterior blends almost seamlessly with the landscape (as shown on page 20), the interior, too, is designed to relate to the natural environment (a goal it shares with the midcentury ranch). Stone accents and horizontal expanses of windows paired with unobtrusive, low-slung furnishings all allow nature to become an integral part of the space.*

OPPOSITE: *The built-ins and other furnishings employed here are prime examples of midcentury design, yet the room seems thoroughly contemporary. While the use of color on the walls and a neutral carpet contribute to the refined yet relaxed look, this room is a testament to the eloquence of modern style.*

OPPOSITE: *True to modernism's main tenets, the gathering areas in this enormous space are defined by partitions and the orientation of the furnishings. The open loft is a clever means of maximizing the functional nature of the existing space.*

ABOVE: *The impact modernism made on room design continues to be felt long after the style's inception. Here, a sitting area in a contemporary home is defined as a distinct space, thanks to a slight shift in levels. Not only is the living room elevated on a small platform, but also its ceiling is higher than that of the adjacent area.*

OPPOSITE and ABOVE: *The California home of prominent midcentury architect Rudolph Schindler embodies all the lessons of room design that modernism has to offer. Furnishings are minimal, thereby calling attention to the spacious feeling of the open floor plan. Vast windows and sliding glass doors contribute to the sensation, ushering in an abundance of natural light and merging the outside environment with the indoor decor. In fact, Schindler wrapped the structure around outdoor courtyards, creating intimate outdoor spaces that are vital and functional parts of the home.*

ABOVE: *The maxim "less is more," coined by Mies van der Rohe, applies here. The soaring space is punctuated by just two pieces of furniture, a diminutive stool and a stylish chaise longue, which was designed by Le Corbusier, Charlotte Perriand, and Pierre Jeanneret.*

OPPOSITE: *Although clearly contemporary, this room has borrowed many design components from the midcentury room. The walls are free of moldings, thereby giving the space a streamlined look, and the hearth is elegantly spare. Plus, there are plenty of floor-to-ceiling windows (though they include the more traditional mullions and panes) to make the most of the scenery outdoors. Combined with a few pieces of Teak Style furniture, these architectural elements imbue the room with a decidedly midcentury tone.*

ABOVE: *In this vast room, lined with sliding glass doors and floor-to-ceiling windows, a fireplace slyly serves as a partial divider between two sitting areas. In keeping with the minimalist look of modern design, the space sports only a few furnishings, including a George Nelson Platform bench (1946) and an Eero Saarinen Womb chair (1946).*

OPPOSITE: *Two steps up, at the other end of the elongated space, is yet another living area. This one encourages free-flowing conversation, thanks to the arrangement of the Eames sofa and molded plywood chairs around an Eames Surfboard table (1951). Note how the wall behind the sofa stops a good distance short of the ceiling, thereby maintaining a sense of fluidity.*

LEFT: *Clean-lined and demure, the floating ledges prevalent in modernist design can be incorporated into virtually any setting. In this small entrance area, the space-saving device performs the service of a console table.*

OPPOSITE: *Alvar Aalto's 1947 birch chair creates a dynamic effect against a low, perforated barrier and an airy partition of floor-to-ceiling poles, which delineate a stairway. The chair's ingenious combination of curved and linear strokes helps balance the two architectural elements.*

OPPOSITE: *Stainless steel cabinets and linoleum flooring, which were advocated by the modernists, revolutionized kitchen design in the 1930s and 1940s. These innovations also made life much easier, since both materials were so simple to clean. Even if a house was strictly traditional, it usually sported a kitchen that was more akin to this aesthetic.*

ABOVE: *The cubic spaces that run into each other in this home pay homage to modernism, even though the structure is contemporary. Instead of separating the living and dining rooms with a wall, the owners have used a screen, painted a soft shade of blue, as a partial divider. As a result, a sensation of continuity is maintained.*

ABOVE: *While this semiformal dining area calls to mind the breakfast nooks of the 1950s, it takes the form to new heights. The banquette looks elegant rather than kitschy. The storage system resembles those from the period, but manifests a few new twists, such as frosted glass shelves and wood veneers that fit together like pieces of a jigsaw puzzle. The table sports a graceful base reminiscent of Eero Saarinen's designs.*

OPPOSITE: *Replacing traditional walls and doorways, a change in level often helped to give individual spaces definition in the open-plan midcentury home. Here, a living area is a half level higher than the dining area, which gives each space some privacy, despite the fact that they flow into one another. The placement of the rug and Teak Style furnishings further emphasizes the distinct identity of the dining area and creates the impression of an unenclosed "hallway" in line with the stairs.*

ABOVE: *Incorporating a flagstone floor, an austere hearth, and sliding glass doors, this living room in a house designed by Richard Neutra is replete with the hallmarks of modernism. Contemporary upholstered pieces blend smoothly with the architecture and the Eames Surfboard table, thanks to the seating's streamlined look. A neutral palette ties the space together.*

OPPOSITE: *The bedroom incorporates just as much glass as the more public areas of the home. Moreover, the expanses of glass remain free of fussy window treatments, allowing the room to bask in the splendor of nature.*

OPPOSITE: *Debuting in the midcentury home, wraparound floor-to-ceiling windows were made possible by the use of steel and concrete supports. In this minimally decorated but comfortable bedroom, the windows are even more sophisticated, rimming parts of the room and showcasing a handsome hearth. The use of glass not only brings residents closer to nature, but turns the entire space into a sculptural work of art in its own right. The floating sensation of the shelf to the left is heightened by the backdrop of sheer glass.*

RIGHT: *The modernists were inspired by the spare lines of Japanese architecture and design, as well as the notion of bringing the outside in. The shower in this master bathroom, designed by Richard Neutra, manages to blend both and still maintain privacy, thanks to a brick wall that graciously shields the space from the rest of the garden.*

CHAPTER THREE

PRIME PIECES

The development of modern furniture parallels that of modern architecture and technology. In fact, many leading designers of modern furnishings were initially trained as architects. Some turned their attention toward furniture when World War II basically brought building to a halt, while others sought to create pieces that would do justice to the new types of homes they were designing. Unlike the days of the craftsman, when an individual would both design and craft by hand his own works, modern furniture relied upon the pairing of a designer and a manufacturer.

Two of the leading U.S. manufacturers of the day were Herman Miller and Knoll International. Herman Miller, based in Zeeland, Michigan, was owned by D. J. DePree, who had started at the company (then called the Star Furniture Company) as a clerk, eventually taking it over in 1919. At that point, he renamed the firm after his father-in-law and business partner, Herman Miller. DePree's first designer was Gilbert Rohde, who joined the company in the 1930s and persuaded DePree to go modern. The line Rohde designed set Herman Miller on a course of producing functional and unpretentious but well-designed furniture. When Rohde died in 1944, DePree hired a new director of design, Yale architect George Nelson, who in turn lined up such visionaries as Charles and Ray Eames and Isamu Noguchi. Nelson also created his own designs, many of which are still in production today.

Knoll International was founded by Hans Knoll, whose father had produced the designs of Walter Gropius and Mies van der Rohe in Germany. Knoll opened a showroom in New York in 1942 and came up with the then novel concept of producing the designs of various talents and paying them royalties. With this tack, he attracted an international stable of designers, including the sculptor Harry Bertoia and the architects Jens Risom, Eero Saarinen, Mies van der Rohe, Le Corbusier, and Marcel Breuer.

While Herman Miller and Knoll were the most prestigious companies producing modern furniture in the United States during the 1950s, other manufacturers included Dunbar of Indiana and Widdicomb, which featured the works of Edward Wormley and T. H. Robsjohn-Gibbings, respectively. And in Western Europe, where modern furniture was also

OPPOSITE: *Though some pieces of modernist furniture are not very comfortable, form and function come together in the Womb chair, designed by Eero Saarinen in 1946. Named for the security it gives its occupant, the chair is constructed of a molded plastic shell, a steel rod base, and an upholstered seat with an additional cushion for lumbar support. The lightweight materials provide comfort sans the bulk usually associated with an easy chair.*

In fact, on both sides of the Atlantic designers and manufacturers were experimenting with new production techniques and industrial materials, such as steel, aluminum alloys, curved plywood, plastics, rubber, foam, synthetic resins, fiberglass, and wire. The principle attractions of these materials were their strength, reasonable cost, and ease of use, and many were utilized in combination. For example, George Nelson's Coconut chair brought together a variety of elements with its molded plastic shell, foam cushioning, and metal frame. For the most part, the results were lightweight, mobile, and sturdy pieces, bearing graceful lines and demonstrating a purity of form. And many furnishings were multipurpose, offering the utmost in function and style.

L E F T : *While modernist chairs have definitive personalities, the linear nature of their designs allows them to fit appropriately in many different contexts. In this hallway, some very early pieces prove the point. Josef Hoffmann's steam-bent wood chairs (at left), produced by Thonet, and a Frank Lloyd Wright chair designed for the Imperial Hotel in Tokyo coexist peacefully, playing off complementary artwork and a period storage unit.*

O P P O S I T E : *Designed in 1956, the Eames lounge chair and ottoman has become the twentieth century's version of the gentleman's club chair. Its composition is deceptively complex. Separate wood forms, each composed of a five-ply molded wood shell with a rosewood veneer, are connected with aluminum and rubber shock mounts to achieve maximum flexibility. The arms are made of steel plates bonded with foam pads, and the whole piece is upholstered in leather or fabric. Last but not least, the chair is mounted on a five-prong pedestal base for stability.*

all the rage after the war, such companies as Cassina, in Italy, and Fritz Hansen, in Denmark, rose to meet the demand for functional modern furniture. Scandinavia and Italy were the most dynamic centers of design in Europe, but many of the stylish Italian furnishings were too expensive to ever make their way to the United States. However, such Scandinavian designers as Alvar Aalto, Bruno Mathsson, Hans Wegner, and Finn Juhl made an international impact on modern furniture. Though they promoted the use of wood and developed Teak Style furnishings, they also explored industrial materials, as evidenced in the designs of Arne Jacobsen, famous for such pieces as the Swan chair and Egg chair, and Verner Panton, noted for his various Cone chairs, among other works.

ABOVE: *In this living room, Arne Jacobsen's Egg chair, designed in the late 1950s for the lobby of the Royal Hotel in Copenhagen, keeps company with pieces of several other periods, including a frothy French Directoire chair of eighteenth-century design and an upholstered sofa. The lively fabrics on the sofa and antique chair play off the vibrant hue of the Egg chair and serve to unify the mix. Ironically, the milieu is anything but minimal, though Jacobsen's designs were notably so.*

OPPOSITE: *In this spacious contemporary living room, a George Nelson Platform bench effectively bridges the divide between svelte tubular steel and leather chairs from the 1950s and a plump overstuffed sofa from the 1990s. The bench's neutral hue and smooth lines make it a highly effective element of transition.*

ABOVE: *Mies van der Rohe's Farnsworth House (the exterior of which appears on page 21) makes the perfect showcase for his furniture. Two Tugendhat chairs—spaced a substantial, but not unfriendly, distance apart—face in toward the center of the space. The Tugendhat chair, which comes in many variations, is named after the family for whom it was originally designed in 1930. Perhaps the most comfortable chair by Mies, it is perennially popular. The couch, also designed in 1930, was the first piece by Mies to incorporate both wood and metal for the frame (steel legs are screwed into hardwood). Ironically, this wholly modern piece of furniture is modeled after an ancient couch design.*

RIGHT: *Usually upholstered in black or tan leather, Mies van der Rohe's 1930 couch goes from austere to sensuous in pure white, lending a space an entirely different tone. Paired here with a bright red Eero Saarinen Womb chair, the piece creates an exciting sense of drama.*

OPPOSITE: *Designed to serve multiple functions, George Nelson's Platform bench can be used as seating or a coffee table. Nelson also put two or three of these together, in a row, to serve as the base for a media center. In this eclectic sunroom, a colorful area rug, filled with rectangles that echo the shape of the bench, helps call attention to the subdued piece. The glass top is a protective contemporary addition.*

ABOVE: *Danish furniture designers of the 1950s often used teak, a superior hardwood that was reasonably priced at the time on account of surpluses in the Philippines. Such Teak Style furnishings were extremely popular in both the United States and Europe. Thanks to the burnished tones of the wood, these pieces look much warmer than most other modern furnishings, as seen in this living room. The warm tones work with the biomorphic shape of the sofa and the nubby upholstery to create an especially welcoming space.*

OPPOSITE: *George Nelson's Marshmallow sofa, which was initially produced only from 1956 to 1965, has been in such demand by collectors that Herman Miller decided to reissue it in 1999. Despite appearances, it is quite comfortable. In this living room, the sofa teams up with an Eames fiberglass chair, in coordinating blue, and a classic Isamu Noguchi coffee table (1947) to add a great deal of spirit to the space.*

RIGHT: *Bold primary colors worked well for midcentury furnishings because of the pieces' simplicity and elegant proportions. These striking shades of yellow would be overwhelming on a less graceful chair, and far less effective on a cabinet made of more luxurious materials. It takes only a few key accessories—the right pillow, painting, and vase—to tie the space together.*

ABOVE: *Many of the pieces produced by furniture manufacturer Herman Miller, but designed by different people, were meant to be used together, even though they weren't specifically created as matched sets. Rather, the proportions and materials employed to craft each piece were complementary, and the silhouettes shared a graceful yet playful quality. In this living area, George Nelson's Platform bench mingles happily with molded plywood chairs, a sofa, and a Storage Unit, all designed by the Eameses. An area rug boasting bold geometric shapes provides a substantial dose of period pizzazz. Fortunately, Herman Miller has recently reissued a number of its "retro" furnishings, enabling home decorators to bring a bit of the not-so-distant past into their rooms.*

ABOVE: *With its sleek, surfboard-shaped profile, this Eames coffee table blends the restraint and excitement that personified fifties design. In this living room, the black laminate coffee table is joined by a George Nelson cabinet and non-swiveling interpretations of Arne Jacobsen's Egg chair, all of which imbue the room with a unified look.*

ABOVE: *Although Arne Jacobsen's Ant chair was designed in the 1950s, it looks right at home in this thoroughly contemporary setting, where it is paired with an Italian desk that rolls along a ledge in the wall. Thanks to the chair's lightweight construction, it too is highly mobile. The desk could double as a dining table with the help of additional chairs.*

OPPOSITE: *This 1952 desk may look like an all-American example of midcentury furniture, but it is actually the work of French designer Jean Prouvé. A chair designed by American Norman Cherner (for Plycraft in 1956) makes the perfect mate, thanks to its similarly angled legs and airy styling. The pairing emphasizes the fact that modernist design has not only spanned decades, but also continents.*

LEFT: *A modernist setting doesn't have to be cold and pristine. This dining suite, which includes the Eameses' molded plywood chairs, becomes warmer and more welcoming thanks to the richly hued carpet and a tall, yellow vase of tulips.*

OPPOSITE: *Thanks to their unpretentious lines, many modernist pieces can work comfortably with furnishings from a wide variety of styles. Arne Jacobsen's stacking chairs (1955) are a perfect example of this versatility. They not only look at home with such pieces as an Arts and Crafts bookcase, Victorian chairs bearing an Art Nouveau tone, and a colorful kilim, but they also give a sense of balance to the diverse mix. A simple modernist table facilitates the integration.*

OPPOSITE: *Such pioneers as Marcel Breuer and Charles and Ray Eames introduced furniture designs that used industrial materials in fresh and imaginative ways. For instance, Breuer employed steel tubing for chairs, and the Eameses combined aluminum, plywood, and masonite panels for their shelving systems. These ideas were borrowed by other designers, who created their own equally interesting variations, such as the pieces shown here.*

ABOVE: *Given the contemporary-looking profile and current popularity of Mies van der Rohe's Brno chair, it's hard to believe that the piece was designed in 1929. Mies created it for a dining table in the Tugendhat house in Brno, Czechoslovakia, but Philip Johnson glorified it when he used it in the interior of the Four Seasons restaurant in New York City. The chair wasn't actually mass-produced until 1960.*

LEFT: *Designed in 1925, Marcel Breuer's Laccio side table was produced in several different sizes that could be stacked together to become all the more striking and serviceable. Although the set pictured here is accompanied by period accessories, namely the pitcher and bedspread, it is strong enough to make a powerful modern statement all on its own.*

OPPOSITE: *The energy radiating from a suite of red upholstered pieces, all of the same modernist vintage, is tempered by restricting the room's color scheme to two hues—red and white. Pieces of contemporary art are dramatic yet perfectly in keeping with the tone of the space.*

ABOVE: *Equally at home in an office or a residential space, this Eames chair is from the husband-and-wife team's Aluminum Group (1958). Thanks to the platform bed's neutral appearance, it can easily be dressed up or down. At the moment, boldly colored pillows add pizzazz to the spare surroundings.*

OPPOSITE: *A piece of modernist furniture can provide the perfect counterpoint in almost any setting. Arne Jacobsen's Ant chair is such an exotic yet spartan piece that it meshes perfectly in this exuberant postmodern bedroom. It also lends the space some seriousness and depth without being too sober.*

OPPOSITE: *Modernist trappings lend themselves to the mix-and-match game. Here, a sleek wall of built-ins is paired with a custom-built vanity that resembles a George Nelson credenza. Decorative accessories, including ones that are authentic and others that are simply evocative of the period, complete the milieu. However, it is the translucent paneling on the right wall that really gives the space an edge. This stylish element calls to mind Japanese shoji screens and the fiberglass panels that were prevalent in the 1950s.*

RIGHT: *A close-up of the sink area shows how a touch of tradition, even a subtle one, can warm up a modern setting. Notice how the gilt-framed mirror plays off the burnished honey and brown tones of the vanity below, yet actually broadcasts and emphasizes the modern elements of the space by reflecting the tile walls and glass vases.*

CHAPTER FOUR

MODERN ADORNMENTS

The distinctive modernist furnishings did not have to go it alone. There were plenty of equally impressive decorative accessories to enhance midcentury homes. Taking on forms and characters that differed from their predecessors, these decorative items broke new ground, in much the same way that modernist architecture and furniture design did. For instance, some accessories were streamlined and spare, just like the open-plan spaces they adorned, while others were asymmetrical, free-form, and curvaceous, mimicking the biomorphic nature of many of their furniture counterparts. Still others were downright kitschy and outrageous, ultimately becoming unforgettable icons of the era.

There were many other ways in which design ideals of the day manifested themselves in decorative objects. Clocks lost their solid faces and took on a range of abstract shapes; the most infamous of these were the "atomic" silhouettes, designed to mirror scientific developments of the time. Amoeba, boomerang, and kidney bean shapes showed up in many incarnations, including lamps, textiles, and vases. Glassware—especially some of the handblown pieces from Scandinavia, Italy, and Czechoslovakia—became witty, organic-looking, and oftentimes colorful. Textiles were woven with nubby

textures or covered with idiosyncratic patterns that made them perfect counterpoints to the clean, spare ethic of the era. Even radios and televisions were not immune, taking on shapes that paid homage to the innovations of the day.

Ironically, many of the items sporting curves or fantastic biomorphic shapes were made not of natural materials but industrial ones—by-products of wartime research and development. The aircraft industry had devised new ways of molding plastics and aluminum, while the automotive industry had developed spot-welding techniques for joining wood to metal, rubber, and plastic. There was also an array of new lightweight materials, such as fiberglass, cast aluminum, acrylics, and resins. All of these substances were absorbed by the

OPPOSITE: *Rife with midcentury accents, this room evokes a feeling of nostalgia while maintaining a fresh appearance. Floating shelves appropriately display a collection of colorful period glass vases and bowls, while a graceful Ericofon telephone rests on the desk. The throw and pillow add texture to the smooth lines of the space.*

decorative realm, where they were often combined with more traditional materials to create novel accessories.

Tabletop pieces, in particular, acquired a sharply midcentury look. Russel Wright, who initially designed furniture for Conant Ball Company, turned his attention toward ceramic, glass, plastic, metal, and spun aluminum, creating streamlined yet sinuous dinnerware that is highly coveted today. His designs for tabletop pieces and other accessories, such as spun aluminum torchères, were produced by many different companies, as well as under his own label, American Way. Another prevalent tabletop line characteristic of the time is Fiestaware. These kitschy, colorful dishes were initially produced from 1936 to 1972 and then reintroduced in 1986. In the Scandinavian countries, tabletop accessories were elevated to an art form. So desirable were the glass vases and bowls of Finnish architect Alvar Aalto that these continue to be produced today. And the lustrous stainless steel and sleek teak pieces crafted in this region are also currently in high demand.

The 1940s, 1950s, and 1960s saw a huge explosion in the production of glass—both for everyday use and for show—thanks to great advances in glass technology. The new capability to make glass resistant to sudden temperature changes opened up a world of possibilities for utilitarian pieces, such as soup bowls, cups, and coffeepots. Plus, manufacturers learned how to produce larger items in distinctive shapes, such as audacious foot-long ashtrays and sculptural pendant lamps. Art glass became particularly popular in Italy, where artisans produced vases, lamps, and sculptures in boisterous forms and riotous tones.

While earlier electric fixtures and lamps had been, for the most part, designed to serve as silent companions to furnishings, this was not necessarily the case during the 1940s and 1950s. Lighting became abstract and figural and far bolder than it had ever been before. Isamu Noguchi's elegant and restrained washi lamps, some of which are still in production today, coexisted with kitschy fiberglass

lamps that sported curiously shaped bases with equally eccentric shades. In short, lighting ranged from sensible to excessive, though the pieces that skillfully blended function and form were the most successful. For instance, Lightolier's slender and highly useful pivotal pole lamps were wildly popular (so much so that other manufacturers began producing knockoffs), and the fixtures of Danish lighting designer Poul Henningsen sported such an ideal balance of substance and style that they have become enduring design icons.

While many midcentury decorative accessories are being produced once again today, there are plenty of originals still out there. There may even be one lurking in your basement or attic.

❖

OPPOSITE: *Midcentury decorative accessories are so distinctive that it takes only a few pieces to make a definitive mark on a space. Thanks to these hanging fixtures, with their biomorphic shapes and bold hues, and an equally curvy vase, a contemporary dining set takes on a fifties demeanor.*

LEFT: *Period accents enhance the modern flavor of this casual dining area, which is furnished with a midcentury table and chairs. A George Nelson Ball clock (1947), so named for the "atom" balls on its spokes, hangs on the kitchen wall, bridging time between then and now. Italian hanging fixtures line up above the counter to shed light on informal meals and snacks while contributing modern zest.*

OPPOSITE: *Such functional accent pieces as Lightolier's three-limbed floor lamp and Charles and Ray Eames's walnut stools (which were made in three variations) were tremendously popular when they were introduced—and for good reason. They were singular accessories that added a huge amount of style and cachet to a space. Although they are shown here with other period pieces, they can lend a fifties mood to any room.*

OPPOSITE: *Interpretations of midcentury styling give this room a period demeanor. A Teak Style dining set, vintage fixtures, and a timepiece reminiscent of a George Nelson Ball clock combine to create a modern ambience.*

RIGHT: *The free-form qualities of protoplasm were often translated into modernist accessories. Alvar Aalto's vases (one of which is shown in white on the shelf) and rugs with curvaceous shapes emulating kidney beans are but two examples of this trend. Clearly, they are powerful pieces, capable of softening the strong, straight lines of many modernist furnishings.*

OPPOSITE and ABOVE: *Boasting clean lines, the contemporary furnishings in these rooms pay homage to their modernist predecessors. Additional tributes appear in the open-plan design of the rooms as well as in the vintage fixtures, including the tall floor lamp sporting a washi shade and the bubble-shaped washi pendants.*

ABOVE: *A 1946 George Nelson desk is made more functional and fashionable by the period accessories that surround it. Sleek Venetian blinds control natural lighting, a starburst clock keeps track of time, and an agile three-limbed floor lamp by Lightolier has all angles covered. The paneled walls and pieces of vintage pottery are also important components that give the setting a bit more polish and verve.*

ABOVE: *Thanks to its simple structure and geometric configuration, an Eames Storage Unit can be used to display either vintage or contemporary decorative objects. In this living room, the panels of such a unit contribute texture, while a Taliesin 2 floor lamp, designed by Frank Lloyd Wright in 1925, adds warmth with its cherry finish.*

ABOVE: *Danish lighting designer Poul Henningsen was opposed to pretentiousness and concentrated his efforts on creating fixtures that merged substance with style. As a result, his lighting devices were straightforward, efficient, and exacting in the sense that they cast a bountiful glow without glare. But above all, they were also graceful and sturdy enough to stand the test of time. The hanging lamps shown here are classics.*

OPPOSITE: *The lightweight, plastic Eames La Chaise (1948) was an experiment designed more for its sculptural form than its performance as truly comfortable seating. Thanks to its unique shape, the piece is a work of art that has great potential to be used as a decorative accessory instead of a functional piece of furniture.*

ABOVE: *Although this room isn't loaded with period pieces, it exudes that impression, thanks to the hanging light fixture that holds pride of place over the dining table. Spun fiberglass produced dramatic effects in lamps during the 1940s and 1950s, as this period piece used in lieu of a traditional chandelier demonstrates. The dining chairs also add some modern panache to the mix.*

A B O V E : *Many pieces designed in the 1950s were smaller and lighter than their predecessors, which allowed them to be used as accessories rather than full-blown pieces of furniture. Because of their size and weight, they could easily be moved around at will. Several cases in point are shown here: Wendell Lovett's Firehood (installed in this room on a concrete platform), a Hans Bellman Tripod side table, and Italian designer Carlo Mollino's cloven-hoof studded white vinyl chair. Floating shelves installed on a flagstone wall hold sculptural vases.*

INDEX

PHOTO CREDITS

3/0.5 (14) 2/05
10/10 (23) 6/10
12/16 28 3/16